At Ease With the Media

At Ease With the Media

A program to help spokespeople

communicate when it counts

Eric Bergman, ABC, APR, MC, FCPRS

Petticoat Creek Press Inc.

Author: Eric Bergman
Executive Editor: Heather Turbeville
Author photo: Alan McKenzie

ISBN: 978-0-9879689-5-1

AUTHOR'S PREFACE

This book was originally published in 2006. At the time, social media were just emerging as viable communication media. As of this writing in mid-2014, we have Facebook, LinkedIn, YouTube, Twitter, Instagram, Pinterest, podcasts, blogs, videocasts, and others.

There is no doubt that we can expect new media to emerge on a regular and frequent basis. However, we should worry less about "traditional" versus "social" media than we should about the distinctions between print and broadcast. We have only two ways to communicate as human beings — the written word and the spoken word — and every communication medium ever invented (or yet to be invented) can be placed into one of those two categories.

If the story for which you're being interviewed will be words on a page or words on a screen, for our purposes we can think of those as "print" media. The route to the end audience is always indirect. There are one or more filters between you as the spokesperson and the audience(s) you'd like to influence. Therefore, the advice provided here for preparing for, and succeeding with, print interviews is directly relevant.

If the story is audio, video, or both, we can think of it as "broadcast" media. Your message and personality must work together. You can talk directly to the audience(s) you'd like to influence (although you cannot and should not ignore the interviewer). People need to get a sense of who you are as a person and a professional before they will buy into your message.

Understand who you're dealing with (whether their story will be print, broadcast, or a combination of the two) and adjust your approach accordingly. The advice here will serve you well.

Finally, two words of caution. First, nothing is ever off the record. That mantra was true 25 years ago, it is doubly true today in an era of smartphones in every hand, security cameras on every corner, and instant access to a global audience through the Internet.

Second, broadcast media are no longer here and gone. In the early 1990s, because of the cost of storing audio and video, unless the story was of historical significance, it was difficult to find it 30 days after it aired. That is no longer true. Stories can now sit on websites for decades, if not lifetimes.

Thank you for purchasing this booklet, and good luck during your exchanges with journalists. The advice here has stood the test of time and, if you keep this preface in mind, will serve you well during your career as a spokesperson for yourself and/or your organization.

Sincerely,

Eric Bergman

TABLE OF CONTENTS

■ INTRODUCTION

Welcome to *At Ease with the Media*. This booklet is designed to supplement the media training workshop of the same name. Together, they will help you become an effective spokesperson for your organization.

The goals of the workshop and this booklet are to provide you with the tools you need to build sound working relationships with reporters. As a spokesperson, your job is to balance the skill of answering reporters' questions with your desire to convey messages that are important to your organization's success. This program embraces a collaborative approach, in which you actively seek ways to meet both parties' needs as a means of creating win-win scenarios wherever and whenever possible. If you can balance these two interests, which are not necessarily mutually exclusive, you can be extremely successful as a spokesperson.

At Ease with the Media has been designed to demonstrate the value of clearly and concisely answering questions. Reporters ask questions for a living. It's a determining factor in why they became reporters in the first place and why they are still reporters today. If you're going to meet their needs, you must hone your ability to answer questions. If you are going to protect yourself and your organization, you must learn to stop talking after you answer those questions.

At the same time, this program is structured to provide you with insight into communicating the logic of your decision making around issues (which are generically referred to as key messages) and weaving those messages effectively into your discussions with reporters (instead of driving them home) as a means of managing issues and crises, defending your organization, raising its profile and/or advancing its objectives.

Why are relationships with reporters important? If your organization is attempting to reach target audiences through the media, or becomes embroiled in a public debate played out in newspaper and magazine articles or television and radio reports, such relationships are invaluable. In fact, virtually every organization today with a public profile and important stakeholders—whether public, private, corporate, non-governmental or nonprofit—will probably need to deal with reporters at some point in its future.

When a reporter does call, you should make every attempt to negotiate about when the interview will take place and what will be discussed. In a straightforward and honest manner, get the time you need to prepare for the interview. Once you are actually in the interview itself, you can control only one small element of it: what you say.

You have no control over the worldview of the reporter. You have no control over the questions asked during the interview. You have no control over who else is interviewed or what additional information the reporter uncovers (although you may influence these by suggesting other people to interview and providing additional background information). Most important, you have no direct control over the final story. This is illustrated by Figure 1, which shows the sources of information that potentially go into any story.

At Ease with the Media has been constructed on the premise that controlling the direction of an interview when you're facing someone who asks questions for a living, by staying "on message" regardless of the questions asked, is a fallacy. Such an approach is not conducive to constructing win-win scenarios, nor is it a proper foundation on which to build positive working relationships with reporters.

This program is based on balance. As a spokesperson, your first objective is to answer questions from reporters wherever and whenever possible. Next, look for opportunities to weave in, not drive home, key messages that are important to your organization's strategic and communication objectives.

FIGURE 1: WHAT GOES INTO A STORY

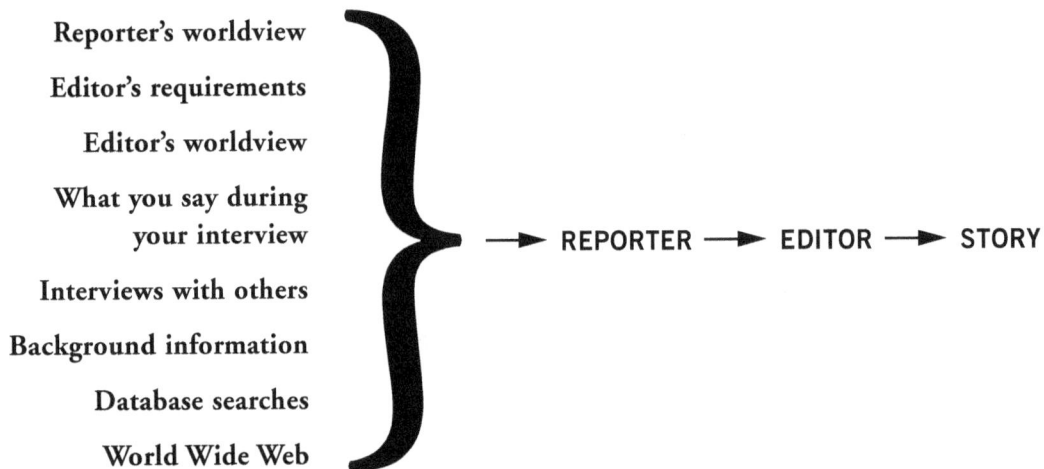

Reporter's worldview

Editor's requirements

Editor's worldview

What you say during
your interview

Interviews with others

Background information

Database searches

World Wide Web

} → REPORTER → EDITOR → STORY

The only thing you can control during the interview itself is what you say. The reporter asks questions, and you answer them. You have the right to play an active role in the process. You can ask for clarification of words and phrases. You have the right to understand the question before answering it. You can challenge prejudicial language. But if you don't answer the questions, reporters will seek the answers elsewhere.

FIGURE 2: THE MEDIA INTERVIEW

A media interview is an interview with any reporter,
editor or other individual for the purposes of gathering a
story for print or broadcast, the outcome of which you will have little
or no opportunity to approve or edit.

While the concepts we examine will assist you if you're interviewed for a story in your company newsletter or magazine, any mistakes you make during internal interviews are easily corrected. You can craft and refine your messages when you review a draft of the article. In a true media interview, the reporter or editor will not seek your approval before the finished product airs or goes to press, and will focus on publishing or broadcasting whatever information they feel will significantly affect the audiences they serve.

STRIVE FOR BALANCE / Your goal as a spokesperson should always be to strive for balance. If you only answer questions, you'll certainly assist reporters, but your organization won't benefit from the time and effort you put into the process. Conversely, if you stay "on message," you'll end up frustrating the reporter. At best, this will make it difficult to build a relationship with that person. At worst, you'll arouse suspicion, and the reporter will leave the interview wondering what you're hiding. If the reporter feels you're hiding something, he or she will begin digging for information. When that occurs, small issues suddenly become large, and your organization may have less success in reaching its communication objectives as a result of your contact with the media.

Sometimes the line of questioning in an interview will go beyond the subject area that was negotiated in advance. If this occurs, try to insert your key messages a few times or try to steer the interview back to the topic area you'd like to discuss (or for which you have prepared). Ultimately, there is no harm in trying once or twice. However, if the reporter brushes those messages aside and ignores your attempts to change the subject, you'll have to make a decision. Do you stop answering questions and keep repeating your key messages? Or do you answer the reporter's questions and save the messages you've prepared for another day or another interview?

This program advises the latter. If you answer the reporter's questions, the interview becomes an extension of your media relations activities, which have, at their core, a need to build some form of relationship with journalists. This is why it's called media *relations*; you want to build relationships with those who have the power to reach audiences important to your organization. If you answer questions effectively, you help reporters do their job. In the future, they will turn to you again as a source of information, and you will get more opportunities to convey your messages.

BEING MISQUOTED / During media interviews, people often fear being misquoted, or having what they say quoted out of context. The reality, however, is that these fears are somewhat misguided, if not misplaced. Today, in the interest of both speed and accuracy, even print reporters use tape recorders. With libel laws being what they are, there is a high degree of certainty that what appears in the story was actually something that you, as the spokesperson, said.

So much for being misquoted. That leaves the second fear—being quoted out of context. When someone complains of this, it's tempting to ask one important question: Exactly how much context was there from which the reporter could draw the quotes?

In its early days, the computer industry coined a phrase that could easily apply to media interviews: garbage in, garbage out (GI-GO). If you succumb to the temptation to talk nonstop in response to even the simplest closed question requiring a yes or no answer, you should be concerned about being quoted out of context. Conversely, if you respond to the reporter's questions with clear, succinct and focused answers, and teach yourself the invaluable skill of stopping after you answer the question, you significantly reduce the chances of having bits and pieces of your information strung together in a way that leaves a less than accurate or favorable impression about you or your organization. At the same time, you increase your ability to convey the messages important to your organization. In print interviews particularly, your messages will stand out as usable quotes if they are surrounded by short answers.

Attending the workshop and reading this booklet gives you a range of tools. Hopefully you will apply these tools to becoming focused, clear and, most of all, concise in the information you provide to reporters.

ELEMENTS EXAMINED / During the *At Ease with the Media* workshop, you learned about a number of elements that can make you an effective spokesperson for your organization, including:

- ▶ Understanding the media.
- ▶ Managing polarization.
- ▶ Working with reporters.
- ▶ Answering questions effectively.
- ▶ Preparing for the interview.
- ▶ Knowing your priorities.
- ▶ Applying strategies for success.

The first section of this booklet is devoted to answering the basic question: What is the media? For the purposes of this training session, we divide the media into two categories—broadcast and print—and compare the similarities and differences in the ways information is gathered and disseminated by television and radio outlets, and newspapers and magazines.

The second section of the booklet examines the concept of polarization. In a nutshell, polarization describes how the media attempt to portray opposing sides of an issue from as far apart as possible. The Polarization Model, introduced in this section, provides a platform on which you can manage issues and hostility effectively. With it, you can use media interviews to influence opinion and further your organization's communication goals. This model is not limited to media interviews. It can also be applied to situations involving potential hostility outside of any media interviews you conduct, such as public meetings and forums.

The third section of the program closely examines what it means to communicate with reporters, not through them. You will receive strategies to help you enhance the relationships you have developed, or will develop, with people whose job it is to ask questions, gather information and ultimately convey that information to others. During this section, we explore the skill of negotiating the interview with reporters by examining situations in which you must have information readily available, and knowing when you can and should "disengage" from the interview to ensure that the information you provide is correct and up-to-date.

The fourth section of *At Ease with the Media* provides insight into answering questions effectively. This is, without a doubt, the most critical skill to develop if you hope to be effective as a spokesperson. In our daily lives, when people ask a question, they are looking for one thing: the answer. If the answer is yes, they will want to hear it. This also applies if the answer is no, maybe, absolutely, positively, never or under certain circumstances. This section of the booklet reinforces the importance of the principle less is more, and that being clear, concise and focused in your answers reduces the chances of being quoted out of context.

The fifth section of the booklet provides a model and process for preparing yourself and your messages in advance of the interview. This simple, logical approach will help you develop your thinking, and lead to clear messages for the audiences with whom your organization wishes to communicate.

Sixth, we examine your priorities as a spokesperson. First and foremost, our message is that you protect yourself. This section emphasizes the best way to protect yourself and your organization: to answer questions and stop talking once you have.

The final section of this booklet is devoted to providing simple strategies for success. We examine three basic types of media interviews: print, broadcast sound bites and broadcast live interviews. There are similarities and differences in the ways that each should be handled from your perspective as a spokesperson. And, in this section of the booklet, we reinforce the most striking similarity—you must, at any time, be able to answer the reporter's question as clearly and succinctly as possible, then stop talking. If appropriate, of course, weave in your key messages. But remember, there is a time and place for everything.

By the time you finish reading this booklet, you should have a strong understanding of how the media operates, the needs of reporters, and what you must do to match your needs with theirs.

PART I /
Understanding the Media

In its purest definition, the role of the media is to keep audiences informed—quickly, accurately and to the best of their ability—on matters that significantly affect those audiences. So, you might ask, who decides what "significantly affects" the readers, listeners and viewers of a newspaper, a magazine, a television station or a radio station? Quite simply, that is the job of the editorial staff.

Let's face it, editorial staff—the reporters, producers, news directors and editors who work at various media outlets—are human. They are trained to dig up information, and they have, at some point in their career, been exposed to the idea of journalistic ethics, which means most feel a responsibility to communicate accurate information and both sides of a story. Of course, from their perspective, the further apart the two sides, the better the story.

Reporters, editors, news directors and producers are subject to the same foibles as the rest of us. They are busy. They don't have a lot of time to waste. They may or may not have a history with you or your organization. They are trained to set as many of their personal biases aside as possible, in an attempt to report on a particular issue or situation from a fair and balanced perspective, but like everyone else, they are human.

You cannot control what comes out of this process. You can only control your portion of what goes in. Some would say this means you should stay on message, regardless of the questions asked. This approach is different.

Your first responsibility is to answer questions, then find places to weave in, not drive home, your messages. Your job as spokesperson is to manage the interview process in a way that leads to positive outcomes—a win-win for both parties.

To do this, you must meet the needs of reporters. To meet their needs, you must answer their questions. The paradox of this process is that if you answer their questions and stop, you will be in greater control than ever.

If you do need to take a defensive position, you can focus your efforts on the messages you'd like to send through the reporter to the audiences important to your organization. But, as we'll discuss later, you must use this tactic sparingly and only as a last resort.

BROADCAST AND PRINT—TWO FORMS OF THE MEDIA / The media can be divided into two general categories: print and broadcast. This distinction is made because of the ways information is gathered and conveyed by each medium.

In general, print reporters need more information than their colleagues in broadcast; the first two or three paragraphs of a newspaper article can potentially contain as much depth on a topic as an entire story on radio or television. As a result, print interviews tend to be longer than those for broadcast, and print reporters, by nature, tend to ask more questions.

Because they can show a topic in greater depth, print articles portray issues in subtle shades of gray. Items on TV and radio, especially in newscasts, tend to be more black-and-white because there is simply less time and space available to demonstrate subtleties related to an issue.

Print is a passive medium. If someone reading an article is interrupted, the next word or sentence in the article sits waiting for the person to resume reading. Broadcast is an active medium. If someone is interrupted while watching TV or listening to the radio, he or she may have to wait until the next newscast to get the rest of the story, go to the Internet, or order the tape from a media monitoring outlet.

Print lasts forever. It is possible to go to a library or archive and find an article that was published 10, 20 or even 100 years ago. In broadcast, unless the story is of significant historical significance, you will have trouble finding it as soon as 30 days after it airs.

In print, the reporter may use a quote of yours, but the path to the end audience is always indirect; you communicate with the reporter who, in turn, takes your information, combines it with other information, filters it and communicates it to readers. In broadcast, because of sound bites on TV and actualities on radio, or in the case of live interviews, it is possible to send messages directly to the audiences important to your organization.

It is important that you, as a spokesperson, understand the differences between broadcast and print. If your interview is with a print reporter, know that it can be lengthy. There will be more questions than a similar interview for broadcast. It is possible to show issues in shades of gray, so you can educate the reporter (and, by extension, the readers) about the subtleties of the issue. However, you must be clear, concise and focused in the answers you provide. The best way for reporters to educate themselves is to ask as many questions as possible. Your basic strategy is to answer questions and stop talking, and pick appropriate moments to weave in key messages.

For a broadcast interview, particularly if the reporter's goal is to get a sound bite from you for insertion into the story, the overall interview will be shorter than print. There will be fewer questions, but the reporter will need longer answers from you for each question asked. You will still answer the questions, but you can weave in your messages more often than you would for print.

Figure 3 outlines some of the basic differences between print and broadcast, and it compares the specific characteristics of each particular medium. Following that is a brief description of the four major media types: television, radio, newspapers and magazines.

FIGURE 3: DIFFERENCES BETWEEN BROADCAST AND PRINT

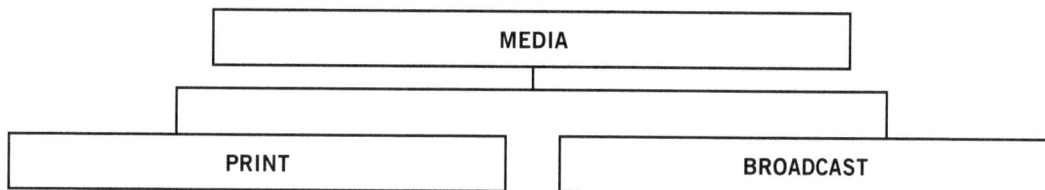

MEDIA	
PRINT	**BROADCAST**

PRINT

▸ Reporters need more information; they as more questions; interviews are longer.

▸ Issues can be shown in shades of gray.

▸ Newspapers and magazines are passive media; the information waits for the reader, not the other way around.

▸ The emphasis is on the message; personality plays little role.

▸ The route to the end audience is always indirect.

BROADCAST

▸ Reporters need less information; they ask fewer questions; interviews are shorter.

▸ Issues tend to be shown as black and white.

▸ Radio and television are active media; listeners and viewers must play an active role in receiving the information.

▸ Message and personality work together in this medium.

▸ The spokesperson can send a message directly to the end audience.

TELEVISION

Today, television is the most influential medium in the modern world. It has high impact, and it is virtually instantaneous. Through the powerful use of images, it has the potential to evoke strong emotion and sway public opinion.

TV news is virtually instantaneous. It has been that way for some time. In the days before the Palm Pilot and Blackberry, when Major-General Lewis MacKenzie, the Canadian staff officer who commanded 14,000 peacekeeping troops in Bosnia-Herzegovina in the 1990s, wanted to relay information to, or request support from, the United Nations, he found it was sometimes "much faster sending the message through the television than by telephone." He simply scheduled a news conference and, by the time he returned to his command centre, a response from the UN was waiting.

Television has the power to raise issues at a moment's notice. It is virtually anyone's tool. Indeed, issues are often selected, and news conferences and other events organized, to meet deadlines for television news.

Television is part information, part show business and part drama. It's part information because the average news item runs less than two-and-a-half minutes (or approximately the first two or three paragraphs of a newspaper article on the same subject). It's part show business because it is rare, for example, to find make-up crews at the city desk of a local daily newspaper. And it's part drama, because drama is created through conflict. The media like to portray conflict through a process known as polarization.

From a media relations perspective, television is an exciting opportunity for you as a spokesperson to convey your personality and message (and, therefore, the personality and the message of the organization you represent). Indeed, those two goals—conveying your message and conveying your personality—are essential to success in making your point on TV. As a spokesperson, you have less than 10 seconds in which to create an effective sound bite—a self-contained unit of information—on television. But to be in control, the trick is to talk less, not more.

RADIO

Radio is a medium of sound. It is similar to television in that it provides the opportunity to combine your personality with the messages you convey. Like television, it also facilitates the opportunity to send messages directly to the audiences important to your organization; the actuality (quote) is radio's equivalent of a television sound bite.

Radio is restricted by the amount of time it devotes to individual news items. But radio can provide 24-hour news coverage and, in an emergency, can be a primary medium of information. Radio summarizes issues and events on regular newscasts. Individual stories average less than a minute (many are 30 seconds or less). However, quotes can last up to 18 seconds, making them about twice as long as sound bites on television.

In addition to newscasts, radio offers a wide array of formats. There is, for example, public affairs programming, which many stations offer and which leads to longer interviews than those done for regular newscasts. These interviews may be conducted in person or by telephone. They tend to last two to five minutes and allow the interviewer to go into slightly greater depth on an issue.

With talk radio, there are two types of programming. The first is the interview/call-in mixture. In this type, the interviewer sets the tone of the program, perhaps interviewing a guest (or a panel of guests), then takes calls from listeners who want additional insight into specific areas of what's being discussed. The second is the pure call-in program. Again, this program may be conducted with a single guest or a panel. This is the most freewheeling format available on radio. The host may broadly outline an agenda, but callers tend to dictate which portions of the outline are to be explored in greater detail.

NEWSPAPERS

Although they lost their pre-eminence as a source of news information as the 20th century unfolded, newspapers still retain a powerful position when it comes to credibility and believability.

Whether a community weekly or a large city daily, newspapers are packed with information. They cover the widest range of topics at the greatest degree of depth. Newspaper reporters tend to ask many more questions than their counterparts in radio and TV; they have to because they require more information to complete their stories as they work toward beating their deadlines.

Newspapers have more opportunities to interpret news than television or radio. Not only can this medium provide a greater depth of information from a variety of sources, but editorial writers and columnists also have the freedom to provide a broader perspective on the issues and topics they cover.

Newspapers command loyalty. People tend to develop close emotional attachments to their newspaper of choice, and they are quick to praise or defend their favorite. Many people don't just read their newspaper. They have coffee or breakfast with it.

Unlike television or radio, newspapers are a passive medium. Information waits for the audience. Finally, newspapers are a record of events. Once it's in print, it's there for all to see; you can clip it, circulate it, file it and look it up on a database two months or two decades from now.

MAGAZINES

Like newspapers, magazines are a passive medium. And, as a general rule, magazines tend not to be as timely. However, the Internet is changing that, at lease for online magazines. The printed versions of magazines operate on production schedules of a few days to a few weeks; as a result, news has already broken by the time magazines get to it.

However, magazines play a vital role in interpreting issues and events. With news as a backdrop, they provide additional insight, often from a human interest perspective. Writers and contributors, both overtly and subtly, express their personal opinions in stories, often combining logic, emotion and a human element to convey powerful images that leave lasting impressions on readers.

Magazines command loyalty. People actively subscribe to a magazine or go through the effort of choosing it from a rack containing many others. Like newspapers, magazines tend to be a permanent record of events. You can go to a library or electronic database to find magazine articles from one, two, or even 50 years ago.

YOUR ROLE AS A SPOKESPERSON / It is important that you understand the role of different media so you can effectively tailor your approach. Print reporters will need more information than their counterparts in broadcast media. They have to teach themselves about an issue before they can turn around and teach others, and the route from you to the end audience—through the reporter, editor and potentially others—is always indirect.

It is critical, therefore, that you are clear, concise and focused during interviews for print media. Your primary strategy should be to pause, answer the question and then stop talking. You will work to find places to weave in key messages. But remember, you weave them in, you don't drive them home.

Broadcast reporters need less information overall but more from you for each question or series of questions asked. In print, you can answer no and stop talking. You can do this occasionally in broadcast, but as a general rule, the reporter will need more information.

PART II /
Managing Polarization

Editorial staff often try to convey polarization in their coverage of events and issues. In other words, the further apart the two sides are in a dispute, the more entertaining the story. This is drama. Drama improves the ratings of television and radio programs, and sells newspapers and magazines.

To understand polarization, it is important to examine the role of issues as a catalyst for defining opinions. An issue is an unresolved problem that has the potential of escalating into a dispute. In the simplest of terms, it is a fight looking for a place to happen. When someone takes issue with your organization, they are mapping out the territory in which that dispute is likely to be fought. Battle lines are drawn, and people choose sides. Figure 4 illustrates this spectrum.

FIGURE 4: THE ISSUE SPECTRUM

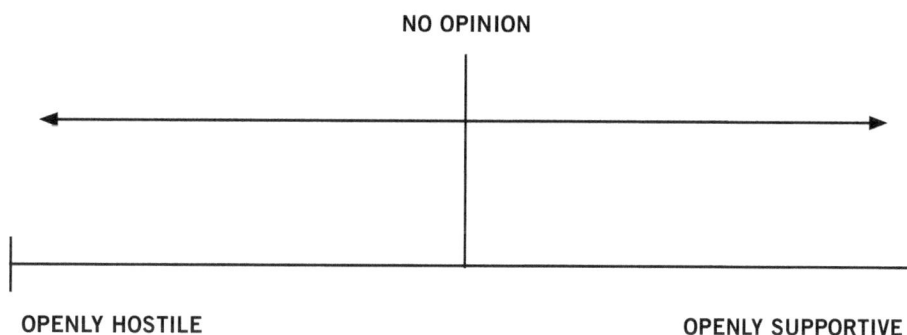

NO OPINION

OPENLY HOSTILE

OPENLY SUPPORTIVE

Along this spectrum, which extends from openly hostile on one end to openly supportive on the other, every potential response to an issue can theoretically be mapped. Those with no opinion are somewhere in the middle and vary in number, depending on the issue.

An example may help illustrate this point: Consider the issue of cutting budgets instead of increasing taxes. On the openly supportive side of the spectrum will be those who strongly believe that any taxation is too much taxation. On the opposite side will be unions, whose members know that smaller government budgets mean fewer government employees, and therefore less union revenue. Between these two extremes, you will find virtually everyone else. Some people may have no opinion about the issue and sit squarely in the middle.

Issues lend themselves to the formulation of opinions. The longer an issue is explored in newspapers and magazines, and on radio and television broadcasts, the more opinions about it form and the more polarization it creates. Going back to the example of cutting budgets instead of increasing taxes, most people, if asked, would prefer to have a few extra dollars, and might favor budget cuts over tax increases. But a significant percentage of the public may also be concerned about how a reduction in government budgets would reduce the level of services they have come to enjoy, or possibly even expect.

The further apart two sides are portrayed in a dispute, the more dramatic the issue and, by extension, the more newsworthy it becomes. News coverage, therefore, tends to focus on the opinionated characters, such as the union representative and the tax activist, or politicians at either end of the spectrum. Our premise is that you can meet your needs and those of the reporter by staying closer to the middle of this spectrum, but still on your side of the issue.

There may be some rare cases in which you or your organization may wish to occupy an extreme position at one end of the spectrum. These must be few and extremely far between if you want to maintain your credibility over the long term. When you respond to someone who has occupied a position on the outer edge, it's important to remember that the middle ground is almost always better. If you can occupy the middle position, the high ground as it is often called, your media interview can become an integral component of your communication strategy.

Figure 5 illustrates this phenomenon. As you move away from the center of the spectrum, people's responses to the issue go from logical and rational to emotional.

What does this mean to you? If you react to emotional hostility with open emotional support, you might have a tasty morsel for the evening news, but there is little chance that anything will be ultimately resolved by the information you convey; you will not change opinions. In watching the news item on television or reading about it in a newspaper, all those who started out on the right-hand side of the spectrum—supporting your perspective—will end up there. Conversely, all those who started on the left-hand side of the spectrum—opposed to your viewpoint—will finish there. Nothing gets resolved.

FIGURE 5: THE POLARIZATION MODEL

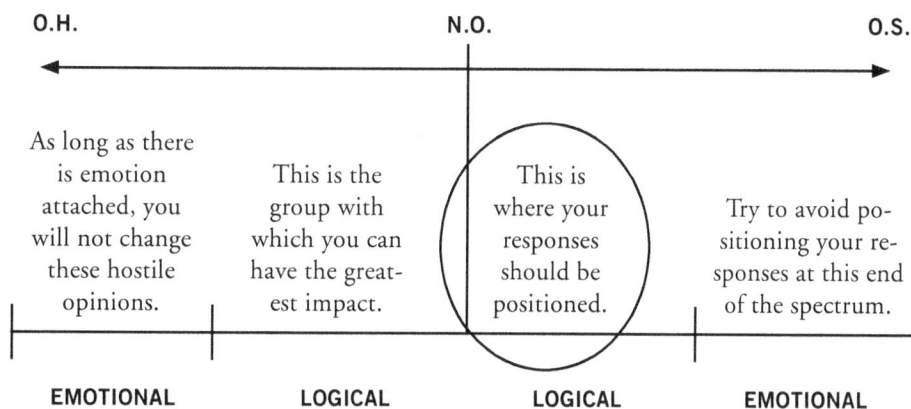

O.H.		N.O.		O.S.
As long as there is emotion attached, you will not change these hostile opinions.	This is the group with which you can have the greatest impact.	This is where your responses should be positioned.	Try to avoid positioning your responses at this end of the spectrum.	
EMOTIONAL	**LOGICAL**	**LOGICAL**	**EMOTIONAL**	

If, however, you can construct messages that are logical, but supportive, you will accomplish a great deal more.

By conveying logical information that supports someone's previously held beliefs, you reinforce opinions that originally supported yours, whether based in logic or emotion. On the other side of the spectrum, as long as someone has an emotional attachment to a perspective contrary to yours, you will never change his or her opinion, no matter how hard you try. So why try? It is appropriate to acknowledge that people have the right to feel the way they do, but not to try to change their opinion by force.

Instead, your responses to the questions asked should be based in logic, fact and reason. If you can achieve this, those with a logical opinion, but one that is opposed to your perspective, are the people with whom you can have the greatest impact. For this group, two forces are at work.

First, if you present a case based on logic, they can compare your logic to theirs and make a reasonable, rational decision. Second, they may become uncomfortable associating with those whose opinions are based in emotion, even if they are technically on the same side of the issue. By offering a reasonable, rational alternative, your view may attract them by offering a means of disassociating themselves from the dissidents and zealots at the outer fringe.

In managing this model, which works as well for public forums as it does for media interviews, it is critical that you answer questions. You must not react to statements. If someone at a public meeting stands up and makes a statement, or a reporter drops a controversial statement into the middle of your interview, you have two choices. You can either thank them for their statement and politely say, "What would you like to ask me?" Alternatively, you can turn their statement into a series of questions and ask and answer them one at a time.

You must pause before answering questions in any situation of real or perceived hostility. Pausing allows you to control your emotions and gather your thoughts.

Finally, you must keep your answers short. This is especially true with print reporters and in public forums. If you cannot stop with a print reporter, you will put yourself in danger of saying too much, which will result in much more context than you would like. With public forums, when those opposed to your perspective get together to discuss what transpired, you want the people with a logical perspective to carry the discussion. You can only do this if you keep your answers short. If your answers are longer than they need to be, those at the emotional end of the spectrum will have all the ammunition they need to twist and turn your words to their advantage later. Keep your answers short, answer as many questions as possible, and you will be able to manage hostility effectively.

HANDLING PERCEIVED HOSTILITY DURING THE INTERVIEW / There are two likely scenarios in which you, as a spokesperson for your organization, may face hostility in a media interview. The first occurs when you feel you must defend your perspective against what someone else has said. The second occurs when it feels like the reporter is actually hostile to you, your organization or the messages you are attempting to convey.

The first scenario most often occurs when a reporter contacts you to tell you what someone else is saying about you or your organization, and asks for your reaction. This is where polarization in the interview begins. The reporter will probably not tell you that someone else is praising your organization. Instead, he or she will present a perspective that is based in emotion, and is completely the opposite of yours.

Your natural inclination will be to respond to someone else's emotion with emotion of your own. But this is where you need to pause and think before you speak. It is also where you will reap the benefits of negotiating the interview with the reporter in advance. You will have taken the time to examine the issues underlying the other group's opinion and to prepare yourself and your messages.

The second scenario occurs when it feels like the reporter is conducting the interview in a curt and impolite manner. This tends to be rare; most interviewers are professional and relatively friendly (although you must never let your guard down; remember that nothing is ever off the record, and the only real friend a journalist has is another journalist). There are, however, some reporters who have a reputation for being belligerent. They use this tactic to "close the sale" and get to the bottom of issues. And there may be times when your organization is facing tough issues.

If it feels as if the reporter is hostile, remind yourself how important it is to pause before responding to each and every question. Use that pause to help you relax as you form an answer before responding. The pause will help you remain disengaged emotionally as you examine each question and develop the appropriate answer. By pausing, you control the pace of the interview, which makes the overall process seem less hostile.

Don't try to meet the reporter head-on. Accept the fact that others may have an opinion different from yours and try to position issues from a positive perspective. And don't respond by using humor. In the best of times, humor can be easily misinterpreted. During a hostile interview, it can be deadly.

PART III /
Working with Reporters

In a media interview, regardless of the issue in question, you will work with a reporter who is trained and paid to ask questions. As you work with that individual, it's important to keep in mind that, overall, he or she is much like anyone else. However, there are some differences between reporters and the general populace. First, they tend to ask more questions than the rest of us. Chances are, they have a natural curiosity and enjoy asking questions, which was probably a contributing factor to them becoming a reporter in the first place.

If you ask them, most reporters will tell you they are overworked and underpaid. Like all of us, they have their good days and their bad ones. They have a job to do, and they've contacted you because they feel you can help them do their job.

Second, reporters universally dislike someone who lies to them. If you develop a reputation as a liar, reporters won't trust you. More than that, they will be less likely to change a negative hypothesis about you or your organization in the future, no matter how compelling the evidence in your favour. And if you ever want their assistance with conveying your good news stories, forget it. They will not have the slightest inclination to help you.

PROVIDING INFORMATION TO REPORTERS / When reporters contact you for an interview, they probably have a good idea of the space that needs to be filled and the type of information that could fill it. They often have in mind a concept of where the various pieces of the story could fit together. They may even have much of the story actually developed. Your job is to help by giving them the information they need and correcting any factual errors while, at the same time, weaving in your perspective in a way that supports your organization's goals, objectives and target audiences.

FIGURE 6: GUIDELINES FOR WORKING WITH REPORTERS

▶ Try to treat reporters like valued customers.

▶ Respond promptly to all inquiries. Make it easy for reporters to do their jobs; they'll appreciate it.

▶ Be impartial from one medium to another and one reporter to another, even though you may like some reporters more than others.

▶ Answer all questions fully, honestly and to the best of your ability. But, at the same time, be brief in your responses. Remember, less is more in face-to-face communication.

▶ Follow through on your commitments. If you promise to get back to a reporter at a certain time, do whatever you can to meet that commitment.

▶ Observe all deadlines. Reporters work to daily and sometimes hourly deadlines. They might not remember you if you help them meet a deadline, but they will never forget you if you cause them to miss one.

▶ Be polite and professional.

▶ Be energetic. Approach the interview with enthusiasm.

When reporters pursue a story, they often follow the scientific method of gathering information. They develop a hypothesis, then find information that either proves or disproves their theory. Most reporters, when they find information that disproves their original hypothesis, will adjust their thinking and develop the story accordingly. In fact, only a small percentage of reporters doggedly pursue their original theory when all available information points to a different conclusion. Having said that, however, it's also important to point out that a high percentage of reporters will become tenacious if they feel you're lying to them or hiding information by obfuscating or evading their questions. If they feel you're not being straight with them, they will keep digging for information. Eventually, they may come up with a skeleton in your organization's closet that will come back to haunt you.

The training reporters receive almost always includes a focus on balance and ethics. This means that those who are professional will present factual information and more than one side of the story. This does not mean that you can confide in them off the record. If you don't want to see the information in tomorrow's newspaper, or watch it on a newscast, don't say it. However, it is important for you to remember a reporter's ethical need for balance and accurate information, because it can often work to your advantage. In striving to provide balance, reporters are obliged to present alternative perspectives on an issue, one of which may be yours or that of the organization you represent.

Reporters have a highly developed sense of the interview process. They know how to ask questions to get to the core of an issue. They can be direct, indirect or oblique. When you accept an interview request, you should understand that you're playing on their turf and, regardless of how high a profile you have or how many times you've been interviewed, chances are the reporter across the desk or on the other end of the telephone has been through more interviews than you. If you ignore a question or sidestep a negative connotation, reporters will spot it every time. You won't fool them. If anything, you'll arouse their professional curiosity.

When you're being interviewed, it's important that you answer questions to the best of your ability, but let the reporter steer the process. There is nothing wrong with weaving your messages into the interview (indeed, it's highly recommended that you do so if you wish to communicate to the audiences important to your organization), but don't try to "snow" the reporter by continually reciting or bridging over to your key messages. If you don't listen and respond to the reporter, you will have difficulty building a relationship with him or her and may, in fact, motivate him or her to quote you out of context.

REAL ESTATE EXAMPLE

Imagine you're in the market for a new home. A real estate agent is showing you a property. "How far is the nearest school?" you ask. "Talking of schools often reminds me of taxes," the agent replies, bridging immediately to the features and benefits of the property. "And the school taxes in this area are among the lowest in the region. That means more money in your pocket, and more money you can save for your children's post-secondary education."

"But how far is the nearest school?" you ask again. "Schools are an important element of any home buying decision," the agent replies, preparing to bridge to key messages yet again, "but so is quality family time after school. One of the features of this property is that it's adjacent to a conservation area. Imagine the walks you'll be able to take with your children after school and on weekends. It's almost like country living, with the convenience of the city."

Finally, you get frustrated: "Can you provide me with the exact distance between this property and the nearest publicly funded educational institution serving students from grades one through six?" This time, the agent completely ignores your question and drives home yet another key message.

Would you find this frustrating? Absolutely. If you're interested in the property, you'll conduct independent research, if for no other reason than to determine why the agent seems to be hiding the distance to the nearest school. Would you purchase the property? Possibly, particularly if it seems to satisfy your other needs and the school is actually located within an acceptable distance. Would you be inclined to nurture a relationship with this agent? Probably not. But some spokespeople (and the consultants advising them) feel they can get away with such an approach in their dealings with reporters.

Don't let this happen when you're being interviewed. Let the reporter steer the process. It is, after all, his or her job to complete the story. Be receiver-driven. Answer questions to the best of your ability. You can sometimes steer the direction of the interview by providing answers that lead to obvious follow-up questions. But remember, when reporters tire of the game, they'll let you know. They'll ask the questions they want to anyway, whether they ask them of you or someone else. And if they ask the questions of someone else, you give up all control in the process because that someone else may have a different perspective or say something that is ultimately damaging to your organization.

IS HONESTY AN OPTION? / In dealing with reporters, especially when you are discussing sensitive or potentially volatile issues, it can be difficult to tell the truth. However, this program advises always erring on the side of caution. When in doubt, come clean. It is better to take your lumps and move on than to lie or waffle your way through an issue.

If you attempt to evade an issue, you can expect it to be noticed. If you lie, and a reporter digs up the truth, you can kiss your credibility good-bye. The reporter will never believe you or trust you again. And make no mistake, reporters talk to each other. If you lie to one, word gets around. If that happens, you and your organization will not be as highly regarded.

If you waffle, do so only when there is absolutely no other option available. Wherever possible, answer the question and tell the truth, no matter how uncomfortable in the short term. Be straightforward and positive. If you or your organization makes a mistake, say so. Correct that mistake as quickly as possible and move on. Use the media interview as a catalyst for creating positive change within your organization, and you will make significant long-term gains, no matter how intense the short-term pain.

FIGURE 7: "DON'TS" FOR WORKING WITH REPORTERS

Don't lie, bluff, exaggerate or pad your answers.

Don't play favorites. Every reporter getting the exclusive will love it; everyone else will hate it.

Don't create barriers for reporters. Make it easy for them to do their job. Hopefully this will turn into good will that gives you the benefit of the doubt when you need it.

Don't be abrupt or rude, no matter how much you feel provoked. The reporter always has the last word when the story comes out.

Don't speculate on the behavior or actions of others. If the reporter wants insights into what prompted someone else to do or say something, politely tell the reporter that you don't feel qualified to speculate, and then suggest that the reporter ask those people directly.

COMMUNICATING WITH REPORTERS / There is no question that you want to communicate through reporters—i.e., use interviews as an opportunity to send messages to audiences that are important to your organization's success. But let's take a moment to clearly define what it means to communicate with a reporter in a media interview, and how talking to them allows you to reach audiences. Figure 8 illustrates a basic communication model.

On one side is the sender in the communication process. The other side represents the receiver. To communicate, the sender encodes a message and sends it out along a medium, where it is decoded by the receiver.

FIGURE 8: THE BASIC COMMUNICATION MODEL

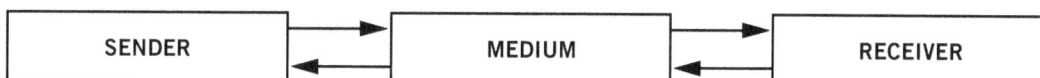

SENDER	→ ←	MEDIUM	→ ←	RECEIVER

But communication, by definition, must be a two-way process. In other words, communication does not actually take place until the receiver acknowledges receipt of the message, encodes a return message and sends it back, where it is decoded by the original sender.

During the interview, the receiver (reporter) asks questions, which the sender (you, as the organization's spokesperson) answer. Even if you're hosting a news conference at which you make an initial statement, you can expect reporters to ask questions. In all cases, with the possible exception of those rare instances when you are dealing with highly volatile issues and you want your single statement to be your only position "for the record," your job is to answer each question as it is asked. In highly volatile situations, you may simply repeat one or two key messages, regardless of the question asked. But use this tactic sparingly, as it may have a negative impact on your long-term credibility and your ability to build positive working relationships with the reporters in attendance.

The basic model illustrated in Figure 8 represents only a portion of what takes place during a media interview, particularly during an interview with a print reporter. Figure 9 illustrates how a reporter, as the receiver of the information you and others provide, takes this information and becomes a sender when he or she develops the story.

FIGURE 9: COMMUNICATING WITH PRINT REPORTERS

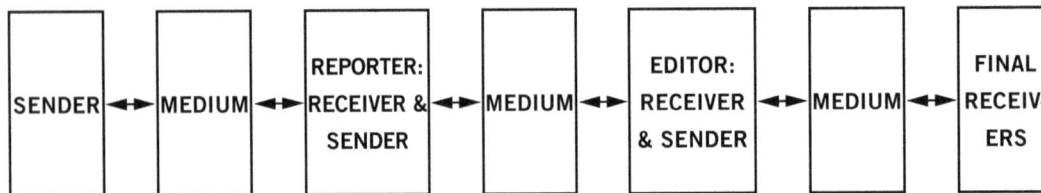

| SENDER | ◀▶ | MEDIUM | ◀▶ | REPORTER: RECEIVER & SENDER | ◀▶ | MEDIUM | ◀▶ | EDITOR: RECEIVER & SENDER | ◀▶ | MEDIUM | ◀▶ | FINAL RECEIV-ERS |

On the left-hand side, the original sender (you, as the organization's spokesperson) participates in an interview with a reporter, who is the receiver. The reporter, however, then becomes a sender. He or she gathers information from a number of sources, encodes it (develops the story), and submits it to an editor for review; the editor then publishes the final story.

This process is often the source of complaints about being quoted out of context. In many ways, it's like the "broken telephone" game where one person whispers a phrase into a second person's ear, who then turns and whispers what he or she heard to a third person and so on. By the time the phrase goes through three or four people, it is no longer recognizable. Getting your message out, especially through print media, is a multi-stage process that, at the very least, includes the reporter and editor. This is why it is vital to be focused, clear and concise during your interviews. Remember, the only thing you can actually control during the interview itself is your portion of what goes into the process—what you say.

One additional element to this model that applies specifically to broadcast interviews is illustrated in Figure 10. As with a print interview, you provide the reporter with information, which he or she adds to other information gathered, before developing the final story. However, for no more than 10–20 seconds in a television sound bite (and often in less time), you have the opportunity to communicate directly to audiences important to your organization.

FIGURE 10: COMMUNICATING THROUGH BROADCAST

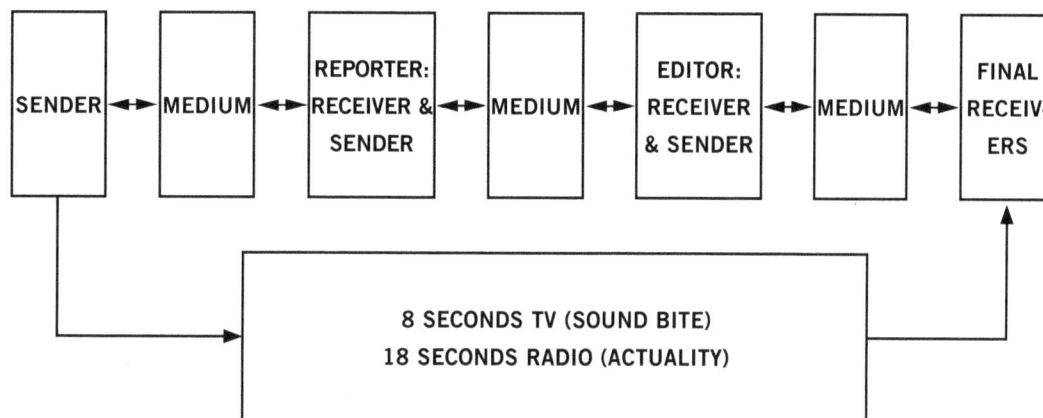

```
┌────────┐   ┌────────┐   ┌──────────┐   ┌────────┐   ┌──────────┐   ┌────────┐   ┌────────┐
│        │   │        │   │ REPORTER:│   │        │   │  EDITOR: │   │        │   │ FINAL  │
│ SENDER │◄─►│ MEDIUM │◄─►│RECEIVER &│◄─►│ MEDIUM │◄─►│ RECEIVER │◄─►│ MEDIUM │◄─►│ RECEIV-│
│        │   │        │   │  SENDER  │   │        │   │ & SENDER │   │        │   │  ERS   │
└───┬────┘   └────────┘   └──────────┘   └────────┘   └──────────┘   └────────┘   └───▲────┘
    │                                                                                  │
    │         ┌──────────────────────────────────────────────────────────┐            │
    │         │          8 SECONDS TV (SOUND BITE)                        │            │
    └────────►│         18 SECONDS RADIO (ACTUALITY)                      │────────────┘
              └──────────────────────────────────────────────────────────┘
```

NEGOTIATING WITH REPORTERS / As a general rule, you should take the time to prepare for interviews with reporters. To get this time, you have to negotiate the terms of the interview, which achieves two goals. It ensures that the reporter gets the most current, up-to-date information available, and it helps you prepare messages to weave into your answers at appropriate points.

There are a few exceptions to this rule. First, if you or your organization has issued a news release, you must be ready to answer questions about the release immediately. You've alerted the media, and you should be ready when they respond.

Second, if the reporter is looking for simple, straightforward facts, you may wish to provide that information. For example, the reporter may ask: How many employees do you have? Where are your offices located across the country? How many retail branches do you have?

If you feel comfortable answering such factual questions (and if this is consistent with your organization's media relations policy), by all means do so. However, recognize that you have the right, at any time, to disengage from the interview to double check your information or find out more from others. If the questions stray from the purely factual, you will want to disengage. The time that you negotiate for those tasks will, in all likelihood, be driven by the reporter's deadline.

If you negotiate the interview terms, or if you need to disengage from the interview in order to get back to the reporter with more information, it's important to establish exactly what the reporter is looking for. What are the topics to be discussed or the issues to be addressed?

Ask the reporter if he or she has spoken to anyone else about the issue. If so, and if the reporter doesn't mind your asking, find out their perspective.

Some other questions you may want to ask include:

▶ What is the space the story will need to fill?

▶ How many words, for newspaper or magazine articles?

▶ How much time will it occupy on TV or radio?

This helps determine the amount of information you'll need to bring to the interview, and will give you a better idea of how long you'll need to prepare. If you're being interviewed by a TV reporter for a regular newscast, you'll need to bring significantly less information than if the interview was a major element of an in-depth newspaper report.

Ask whether the interview will be conducted by telephone or in person. You must agree on a location and/or time for the interview. As you're getting this information, also develop a contingency plan in case something comes up. Where can the reporter be contacted if there's a problem? Where can the reporter reach you?

If appropriate, ask the reporter if you can send background information in advance. Try to send that information as soon as possible. But remember, media relations operates on two important principles: garbage in, garbage out and less is more. Provide appropriate background information as early as possible in the process, but don't throw a mountain of information at the reporter. Be extremely selective with what you send. Strike the right balance, and you will have a better informed interviewer who is less likely to make mistakes concerning your industry, your organization or the issues being addressed during the interview.

As a final item, you may consider asking the reporter if he or she has enough sources on this issue. If not, ask if you can recommend experts, other sources or other potential interview subjects.

Figure 11 contains a reference sheet to help you negotiate interviews with reporters. Please feel free to make copies and use this as a reference guide for negotiating the interview whenever a reporter calls.

FIGURE 11: NEGOTIATING THE INTERVIEW

Reporter's name	Media Outlet	Date

‣ What topics/issues would you like to discuss?

‣ What's your deadline?

‣ Have you covered this issue before? If so, when? Where?

‣ Who else are you talking to about this issue?

     ‣ If you don't mind my asking, what is their perspective?

Type of space/time slot needed to be filled:

TELEVISION	RADIO	NEWSPAPER	MAGAZINE
❑ Newscast	❑ Newscast	❑ Hard news	❑ News magazine
❑ Feature item	❑ Feature	❑ Feature (section)	❑ Trade magazine
❑ Long segment	❑ Interview/call-in	❑ Word count _____	❑ Word count _____
❑ Live interview	❑ Live interview		

‣ When is the item expected to be aired/published?

‣ How would you like to conduct the interview?

    ❑ In person   ❑ By telephone

‣ Where would you like to conduct the interview?

    ❑ My location   ❑ Your location   ❑ Address: _____

    _____

‣ When would you like to do the interview?

    Day_____ Date_____ Time _____

‣ How do I reach you if something comes up?

    Work _____ Home_____

    E-mail _____ Fax _____

Some other issues to work out in advance:

▶ How can the reporter reach you (if necessary)?

▶ Obtain the correct spelling of the reporter's name (and media outlet) if needed.

▶ Recap the issues to be discussed.

▶ Can you send background information in advance?

▶ Does the reporter have enough sources? Can you recommend someone?

PART IV /
Answering Questions Effectively

Answering questions effectively is a critical skill for a spokesperson. Reporters ask questions to gather information. As a spokesperson, your job is to answer those questions. If you ignore the question, evade it or waffle in any way, the reporter will spot it. At the very least, their professional curiosity will be aroused. At worst, your inability to answer the question will affect your credibility as a spokesperson.

If someone asks you what time it is, you probably look at your watch and tell the person. You don't say that it's your favorite watch, that it represents an important turning point in you and your spouse's relationship with your children, that three years ago between 27 July (which is your spouse's birthday) and 4 August (which is your birthday) you and your spouse left your children alone for the first time while you went out for dinner to celebrate your respective birthdays, and that while you were out you walked past a jewelry story and ultimately purchased the watch as your birthday present.

The person asking a question is not looking for a speech or presentation. He or she is not looking for the answers to the next 20 questions that may or may not be asked. He or she wants the answer to that specific question. If the person wants more information, he or she will ask, particularly if you facilitate a communicative environment in which the person feels comfortable asking questions.

Reporters constantly face tight deadlines. They don't have a lot of time to waste, and they don't have a lot of patience for people who can't—or won't—answer their questions. If you're more focused on repeating key messages than finding a balance that allows the reporter to do his or her job quickly and efficiently, you significantly decrease your chances of building a positive working relationship with that reporter.

Although there is sometimes no such thing as a simple question or even a simple answer, your role should be to simplify the process as much as possible. Theoretically, every question sits at the apex of a large pyramid of information. There can be simple answers, as long as you answer only the question being asked, not the 10 or 20 that may or may not follow it. Be accurate, and keep your answers short.

There is no way that you can read a reporter's mind and fully anticipate where he or she is headed with a line of questioning. The last chapter suggested that you get information from the reporter about topics to be discussed when you negotiate the interview. If you do this, you should have an idea of what's coming, but you can't anticipate everything.

During a media interview, remember that this is the reporter's turf. He or she has been on his or her side of the desk, telephone, microphone or camera more often than you've been on yours. Your job, therefore, is to provide focused and clear answers to the questions the reporter asks. It is the best possible way for you to help him or her do his or her job, protect yourself and convey the messages important to your organization.

FIGURE 12: RATHER'S RULES

There are three acceptable answers to every question from a reporter, sometimes referred to as "Rather's Rules," because they are believed to have been coined by television reporter Dan Rather.

▸ Yes, I have the answer to your question, and here it is.

▸ No, I don't have the answer to your question, but I'll get it for you.

▸ Yes, I have the answer to your question, but I cannot provide it at this time.

NOT ANSWERING QUESTIONS / There are a few specific circumstances in which you would use the third of "Rather's Rules" and choose to not answer a question because you cannot currently provide the information. These may be situations in which:

▸ Employees have not yet been notified about a specific issue. Your people shouldn't get the news through a newspaper article or a television or radio report.

▸ Employee, patient or client privacy may be breached by answering the question.

▸ A disaster or emergency has taken place, and next-of-kin have not yet been notified.

▸ Sensitive competitive information would be divulged, which would provide competitors with insight into your sales or market share.

▸ Securities legislation would be breached.

▸ Sensitive union negotiations are taking place, and a "news blackout" has been imposed.

▸ The organization is being sued, and legal counsel has advised against communicating through the media.

When it comes to the last reason for not communicating, "legal counsel has advised against communicating through the media," it's important to use this option with caution. There are two courts in the land: the court of law and the court of public opinion. In the first, you're innocent until proven guilty. In the second, you're guilty until you can prove your innocence.

If your opponent in court is courting the media, it may be vital to prepare a suitable defense in this forum as well. Discuss this with your legal counsel to see if there is a way in which you can defend yourself effectively in the court of public opinion without jeopardizing your legal position.

It is best to disengage from the interview when you don't have the answer to a question. If you're not sure of the answer, don't guess. Tell the reporter you'll get back to him or her with the accurate answer. You will, at that point, be renegotiating the interview. The amount of time you have to find the answer will be based on the reporter's deadline.

PAUSE BEFORE RESPONDING / In general, especially during print interviews and all interviews for sound bite and actuality purposes (and, in fact, in your personal and professional life), you should pause before answering every question. The only case in which you can't pause is the live interview. With the exception of the live interview, therefore, this first pause is a tactic that enables you to:

▸ Take the time to think, examine the question and understand it.

▸ Formulate the right answer (which is almost always the shortest possible answer).

▸ Determine if it is appropriate to weave your organization's message into the answer.

▸ Maintain control over the pace of the interview and your own emotions.

▸ Look confident.

▸ Establish a pattern in which difficult questions will not stand out.

▸ Become a better listener.

Once you've paused, the next step is to answer the question. But remember, you're not answering questions that the reporter may ask in the future. You're not answering questions that you hope the reporter will ask. You are simply answering each question as it is asked, allowing the reporter to steer the process. After all, he or she is responsible for developing the story.

Once you answer the question, and if you have woven in a brief message (assuming this is an appropriate point at which to do so), stop talking. Let the reporter ask the next question. By keeping your answers brief, you can manage the process and find ways to match your needs to theirs.

You should approach interviews from a collaborative perspective. Help the reporter do his or her job. Build a win-win situation if possible. Answer questions clearly and concisely. Stop talking more often than not. Do not passively lie back and accept whatever whim the journalist throws your way. If you have to adopt a defensive posture because the circumstances dictate that you should, do so without hesitation. Your two top priorities are to protect yourself and your organization. Believe it or not, you can often achieve both priorities by simply answering and stopping.

"NO COMMENT"—THE WORST POSSIBLE COMMENT

There are very specific situations in which your organization may choose not to communicate, but there is no situation in which you or another spokesperson from your organization should ever say "no comment." You may choose to tell a reporter that "we do not discuss our sales and profit figures for competitive reasons." You may ignore a reporter's question and substitute your own message (a perilous prospect, but a tool that may be used sparingly). Or you may "decline to be interviewed for the program" because the issue under discussion is before the courts. But "no comment" is not an acceptable answer.

Those two words make a very strong statment about you and/or your organization. As reported in the *Public Relations Journal*, research has shown that an organization that chooses to not communicate by saying "no comment" is believed to be guilty of wrongdoing. In similar research (also reported in the *Public Relations Journal*), a study found that 95 percent of people surveyed were more offended about a company lying about an issue than the issue itself—no matter how bad the issue. This statistic underscores the importance of coming clean.

Remember, no matter how down and dirty an issue seems at the time, all dust eventually settles. Every issue passes. All media spotlights, at some point, will focus on someone or something else.

DIFFERENT TYPES OF QUESTIONS

A reporter's stock-in-trade is asking questions. Like any good professional, a reporter has a variety of tools that he or she brings to the interview. Each of these tools is different, because each is designed to create a different effect. The reporter may be trying to trip you up. More often than not, however, the reporter is probably attempting to draw you out. The purpose of this section is to help you identify some of the tools reporters use, so you can protect yourself.

Remember, the best protection of all is to pause, answer each question as it is asked and then stop talking. This simple strategy will enable you to be clear, concise and focused, and to protect yourself and your organization by controlling what you say.

THE RAPID FIRE ROUNDUP

This tactic is most common in news conferences and media scrums, but it may also occur during one-on-one interviews, especially with a broadcast reporter who is trying to get you to talk long enough to provide a sound bite. A reporter using the rapid fire roundup asks two, three or four questions in a row.

Usually, one of a few things is happening. Either the reporter feels that he or she is only going to have one chance at asking questions and is trying to get them all in with one breath, or he or she is deliberately trying to keep you off balance.

Regardless of why you're being asked a number of questions in a row, it's important to deal with the questions one at a time. If you're unsure of one of the questions, re-word the question and get confirmation from the reporter that this is what he or she is asking. Then answer the question, and determine if this is an appropriate point at which to weave in one of your organization's key messages. If possible, you should also allow the reporter to rephrase any questions that were accidentally missed or skipped as you provided the answers.

THE LOADED QUESTION

This type of question tends to come in two parts. In most cases, the loaded portion is in the first part. When dealing with a loaded question, you must determine whether to address the loaded portion. If so, you must defuse it before answering the question.

For example, suppose the reporter asks, "Given that you've said the former refinery property will always be contaminated, why don't you just turn it into a park?" A possible reply could be: "I didn't say that the land will always be contaminated. Commercial use is still a possibility. So is turning it into a park."

THE DEADLY DOUBLE NEGATIVE

This is similar to the loaded question. It also comes in two parts—neither of which is palatable. You are faced with a lose-lose situation. Deal with this type of question like you would a loaded question and defuse it by "unloading" both parts of the question.

For example, suppose that you're a spokesperson for a software manufacturer and, during the interview, the reporter asks, "You said your software sales are not as good as you expected. Is that a result of bad design or faulty manufacturing?"

You might respond by saying, "Neither. The software itself has received outstanding reviews in trade magazines. If anything, we're guilty of not marketing it effectively."

Answering the question is often the easiest way to deal with this dilemma. In the example above, in which the reporter has just asked if it's a result of bad design or faulty manufacturing, you could simply respond by saying, "Neither." If the reporter wants to know why you feel that way, or what any third option would be, he or she will ask.

THE PERIODIC (OR PERSISTENT) PREGNANT PAUSE

In this situation, the interviewer lets the silence hang as a way of encouraging you to keep talking. People who are inexperienced in media interviews interpret this as a signal to keep talking and, unfortunately, will often say things they wish they hadn't.

Well-known Canadian journalist Peter C. Newman has used a variation of this technique when he wants an interview subject to keep talking. He has been known to fake falling asleep. When he does this, the natural instinct of the person being interviewed is to talk more, not less. Of course, Newman leaves the tape recorder running, and claims to have gotten some of his best journalistic pieces during such sessions.

If the reporter seems disinterested, or pauses, stop talking. Remember that "dead air" is their responsibility, not yours. Considering that reporters are trained to ask questions, you probably won't have to wait long until they ask the next one.

AN EARFUL OF ECHO

This is a tool commonly used by lawyers and psychiatrists. Reporters also use it effectively. It's really not a question at all. The interviewer simply echoes four or five of your words back to you, hoping that you will continue to talk. You need to be aware of this technique and do one of two things: Repeat the reporter's words and use this echo as an opportunity to weave in your organization's message, or close off with a firm statement.

For example, you may tell the reporter that you "hope to have our newest factory up and operating by the end of the year." The reporter might echo back, "By the end of the year?"

At this point, you can do one of a few things. You can say, "That's correct." You can say, "Yes, by the end of the year." Or you might weave in a key message and say, "Yes, by the end of the year. Our goal is to have this facility play a major role in our global manufacturing strategy as quickly as possible."

By closing this process off with a firm statement, you look confident and credible. Remember, if the reporter wants or needs more, he or she will ask.

A TWEAK OR A TWIST

This is very much like the echo, except that when the interviewer repeats a key phrase of the answer, he or she adds a new twist. What comes back is not necessarily what you sent out in the first place.

For example, you might tell the reporter that you're "rescheduling the opening of the new factory for July 15th." The reporter might respond by saying, "You're delaying to July 15th?" "No," you might respond, "we're rescheduling for July 15th. It was the only day the mayor was available."

INFURIATING INTERRUPTIONS

This occurs when the interviewer constantly interrupts you. It seems that you barely have time to get half the answer out before the reporter cuts you off to ask another question.

If this occurs, ask yourself the following:

▸ Are my answers too long?

▸ Am I really answering the reporter's questions?

▸ Am I ignoring the questions and constantly trying to drive home my messages?

If you are responding to the reporter's questions with answers that are short and to the point, you can probably assume that this is the reporter's style, and that it is designed to keep you off balance. To deal with this situation, don't get flustered. Don't try to talk over the reporter. Stay calm. Listen to the questions, and keep trying to answer as best you can. Above all, pause before responding, and keep your answers short.

PART V

Preparing Yourself and Your Message

From the moment you begin negotiating an interview with a reporter, it is your responsibility to ensure that your organization's media relations policy is properly applied. If that policy says you should contact your public relations or communication department when a reporter calls, please do so. Even if it's not stated in your policy, it can be a good idea, whether formally or informally, to consult with your PR department and others as soon as a reporter contacts you for an interview.

You should never operate in a vacuum when preparing. As the spokesperson for your organization, your job is to find the weaknesses that exist in advance of the interview. Your personal reputation is on the line every time you accept an interview with a reporter. Talk to your peers, your coworkers and/or your boss. Consult with your public relations department or media relations representative.

Let each of these individuals know the interview is taking place, and ask them if there is anything you need to know before you are interviewed. It's important that you uncover potentially sensitive areas before the reporter points them out to you.

Try to think of all possible contingencies that could emerge. That way, if the questions do get tough, you'll be better prepared to protect your organization and, just as important, your personal credibility.

Once you've successfully negotiated the interview and have given some thought to the issues underlying any potential disputes, the next step is to gather information and develop messages that you will weave into your answers.

EXAMINE THE ISSUES / To prepare yourself, you must first examine the issues facing your organization, and/or the issues the reporter raised while you were negotiating about the interview. Your next step is to work through a process of developing the logic underlying these issues (your messages) so that you can be prepared to weave this logic into your answers at appropriate moments.

To do this, use the Simple Issues Management Model in Figure 13 as your guide. This model provides a logical, step-by-step approach for developing messages important to your organization's goals and objectives. You should develop no more than three or four messages for each interview; indeed, if it's a taped TV or radio interview for use in a newscast, you might want to reduce that number to one or two messages. If you develop more, you run the risk of spending more energy on weaving in your messages than on answering the reporter's questions.

FIGURE 13: SIMPLE ISSUES MANAGEMENT MODEL

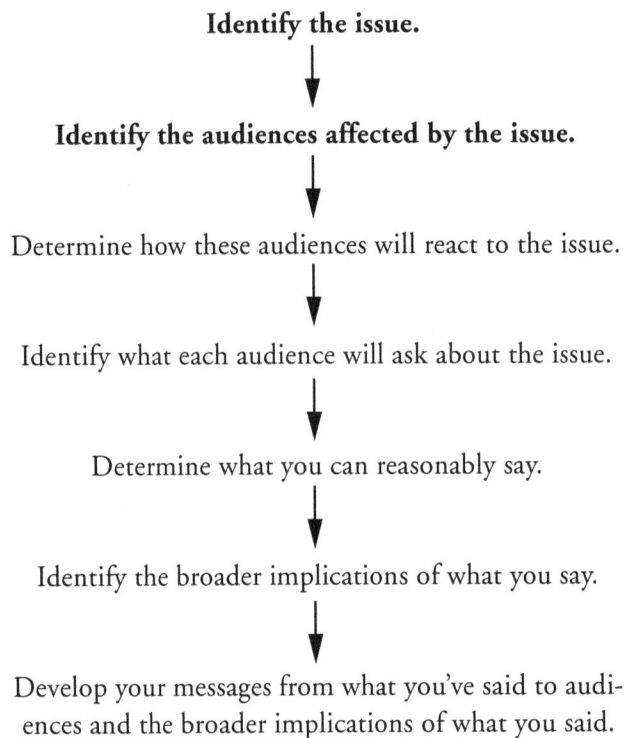

Identify the issue.

↓

Identify the audiences affected by the issue.

↓

Determine how these audiences will react to the issue.

↓

Identify what each audience will ask about the issue.

↓

Determine what you can reasonably say.

↓

Identify the broader implications of what you say.

↓

Develop your messages from what you've said to audiences and the broader implications of what you said.

Remember, your job as a spokesperson is to find the balance and manage the process to a win-win conclusion. On the one hand, you are helping a reporter do his or her job by answering questions. On the other, you are providing messages to the reporter, who you hope will convey those messages to the audiences important to your organization. You must be clear, concise and focused during the interview if you hope to maintain this balance and do your job as a spokesperson.

1. IDENTIFY THE ISSUE

So what is an issue? As discussed in the chapter on polarization, an issue is an unresolved problem that has the potential of escalating into a dispute. It is a fight looking for a place to happen.

When someone "takes issue" with you or your organization, they are mapping out the lines of that dispute. Because issues produce opinions, people line up along the boundaries of the dispute according to the opinions and beliefs important to them at the time.

On your own, or with the assistance of your public relations or media relations department, jot down in one sentence the main issue you will potentially face during the interview (which you identified when you negotiated the interview with the reporter). For example:

▸ As the local school board, we are recommending a 12 percent increase in school taxes for the coming year.

If you're a spokesperson for the school board, such a sentence helps define the battleground on which a potential dispute is likely to be fought. Any time you're planning to raise taxes, people are bound to have an opinion. The next challenge, therefore, is to identify the audiences affected by this issue.

2. IDENTIFY THE AUDIENCES AFFECTED BY THE ISSUE

In *Excellence in Public Relations and Communication Management*, which is perhaps the definitive source of intellectual information about the PR business, James Grunig and his colleagues suggest a very unique method of identifying audiences. Their approach can be effectively applied to the media interview process.

The authors suggest segmenting audiences on the basis of how each specific audience reacts to an issue. Once they are segmented according to their responses, it becomes easier to develop clear and concise messages that will communicate directly to those audiences.

For example, with the school board issue, the openly hostile side is occupied by all those who believe any taxation is too much taxation. On the other end of the spectrum, at the openly supportive side, are those people who believe that the quality of education has suffered as a result of government belt-tightening, and that it is now time to re-invest in young people.

Other specific audiences include:

▶ Parents of young children.

▶ Parents of teens.

▶ Grandparents with children in the local school district.

▶ Grandparents who reside in the local district but whose grandchildren do not.

▶ Politicians at the municipal, provincial, state or federal levels.

▶ Young couples planning to start a family.

▶ So-called "empty nesters."

▶ Others.

Each of these groups will have a different opinion about raising school taxes. Some of the opinions will be similar, and there are some potential audiences—young, single apartment dwellers, for example—who may have no opinion about this particular issue because they feel they have no vested interest in it. Your job at this point is to identify each audience by their reaction to the issue, and then group the audiences accordingly.

For the purposes of this training, we're going to work through audiences comprised of homeowners (primary taxpayers). The assumption is that the more narrowly you can define an audience, the more clearly you can understand their perspective and the more effectively you can communicate with them.

For example, under the broad heading of homeowners, we have:

▶ Homeowners with school-aged children.

▶ Homeowners with pre-school children.

▶ Homeowners planning families.

▶ Homeowners with grown children.

▶ Homeowners who do not have children.

Each of these audiences is slightly different. While there will be similarities in their reaction to an increase in the local school board tax, there will also be a number of differences. The task is to identify the differences in each audience's reaction to the issue and develop the remainder of the model on the basis of those reactions.

3. DETERMINE HOW THESE AUDIENCES WILL REACT TO THE ISSUE

You've identified the issue and the audiences that are directly affected by the issue. Now you need to determine how each audience will react to the issue—whether their opinion is based in emotion or logic, and whether it opposes or supports your organization's perspective.

After listing the audiences, write down beside each audience what you anticipate their reaction to be—either positive or negative (+ or -)—and whether you believe their reaction will likely be based in logic or emotion (l or e), or a combination of the two.

The more narrowly you segment the audiences, the better your chances of understanding how they will react; thus, the better able you will be to craft messages that address their questions or concerns. In the school board example, the reaction of parents with grown children will be slightly different from those who have school-aged children. Each group will have slightly different questions and will require slightly different messages.

Keep in mind the concept of managing hostility with the Polarization Model. If you identify an audience that has an openly hostile opinion on the issue, don't try to meet them head-on. Be aware of their opinion, but focus on those whose opinion is based in logic, whether their opinion supports yours or is opposed to it.

For example, consider homeowners with school-aged children. This group might be opposed to a tax increase (after all, who wants to pay more taxes?), but those in this group will have a logical perspective. Of all the groups, this audience can be counted on to listen to how this increase will benefit their children, and may be swayed by your logical arguments.

4. IDENTIFY WHAT EACH AUDIENCE WILL ASK ABOUT THE ISSUE

Once you determine how each audience will react to the issue, the next step is to determine what they will ask as a result of their beliefs and opinions. The questions they ask are a direct extension of how they feel about the issue. Will they express concern? Could they support your efforts? Do they have strong feelings?

In the school board issue, there are a wide range of potential reactions. Some people at the hostile end of the spectrum might ask, "Why would they think that any new taxation is acceptable?" On the opposite end of the spectrum, people might ask, "How can anyone who is rational not support more money for education?"

If you're a spokesperson for the school board, you should use reasonable, rational messages that are positioned near the middle of the polarization spectrum. These will reinforce both logical and emotional opinions that support yours, yet will be less likely to alienate those whose opinions are based in logic and reason, but different from yours.

Homeowners with school-aged children might ask a number of questions:

▶ Is the increase necessary?

▶ Are other options available?

▶ Where is the money going?

▶ How will our children benefit?

Parents of grown children might ask many of these same questions, and they may also ask, "Haven't we already paid our fair share?"

To complete this module, try to think of questions each audience would ask and write them down in the next column of the model. The next challenge is to answer those questions.

5. DETERMINE WHAT YOU CAN REASONABLY SAY

In most cases, your organization's response and what you say during the interview should be based in fact and focused on those who view the issue from a logical perspective. If you decide to strike back at those who are emotionally hostile to you or your organization, you may solidify opinions among those who originally supported you, and run the risk of driving away everyone else whose opinions are even slightly different from yours. No opinions will change.

Your best approach is to sift through the emotion to locate the facts of the argument, which you will carefully position through reason. Work from left to right on the worksheet. Beside each question, write down a simple, direct answer to the question. For example, homeowners with school-aged children may ask, "Was this increase necessary?" The answer had better be yes. Logically, if the increase was unnecessary, the school board should not be asking for another 12 percent.

This is where sound decision making plays a role in effective communication. Theoretically, if the increase is justifiable at the boardroom table, it should hold up to the scrutiny of a media spotlight. Once you focus on the facts, you can develop rational, reasonable arguments. This position can be tough to maintain in the heat of the battle, but it is your best insurance in using your media relations efforts to change opinions in the long term among those who watch TV, listen to the radio or read newspapers and magazines.

6. IDENTIFY THE BROADER IMPLICATIONS OF WHAT YOU SAY

At this stage, analyze your answers and expand them one small step further, again working from left to right on the worksheet. For each answer you gave, what is the broader implication of that answer to the question?

For example, homeowners with school-aged children asked, "Is this necessary?" After answering yes, the broader implication might be: We cannot take any more resources out of the classroom. The broader implication simply takes the answer one additional step. Again, work through each of your answers in sequence to determine the broader perspective for each one.

7. DEVELOP YOUR MESSAGES

Examine what you've reasonably said to each audience and how you've addressed their concerns. Then look at the broader implications of your statements, which you wrote down on the worksheet.

Once you have worked through this process, highlighted in Figure 14 on page 46, your final step is to write down what you believe are the three or four most important points and their broader implications. Each message should be a note of a few words, not a compound sentence or a complex paragraph. Wherever possible, the messages should be simple statements. You may even have these messages in front of you when you're being interviewed (indeed, if you're being interviewed by telephone, you should always have these messages in front of you).

This seven-step process is illustrated in Figure 14 on page 46, in which a version of the model has been completed for the issue of raising school taxes by 12 percent. A blank version of the worksheet has been provided in Figure 15 on page 47. Please feel free to make as many copies of Figure 15 as you need to develop your thinking, your logic and your messages for future media interviews.

FIGURE 14: MESSAGE DEVELOPMENT WORKSHEET (COMPLETED)

Issue: As a school board, we have decided to increase the school board portion of municipal taxes by 12 percent.

AUDIENCE	EXPECTED REACTION	WHAT WILL THEY ASK?	WHAT DO WE SAY TO THEM?	BROADER IMPLICATIONS/ POSITIONING STATEMENTS
Homeowners with school-aged children	Negative (-)/ Logical (l)	Is this necessary?	Yes.	Without this increase, the quality of education will decrease.
		How much will my taxes actually go up?	About CDN$40 per household per month on average.	This represents about CDN$1.35 per family per day.
		Have you examined other options?	Yes.	We have implemented other options, which is why we haven't had an increase in four years.
		What will this mean to my children?	This increase will go directly to the classroom.	More resources in the classroom means we can maintain quality of education.
		Where will this money go?	To the classroom.	Where it belongs.
Homeowners with pre-school-aged children	Negative (-)/ Logical (l)	What will the system be like when my children get there?	We are committed to quality education.	We will do what's necessary to maintain and, where possible, increase quality.
		When was the last time you had an increase?	Four years ago.	We have managed our increasing costs by becoming more efficient.
		Will you wait this long to bring another increase?	We don't know.	Smaller, incremental increases are something we're looking into.
Homeowners with grown children	(-)/(l & e)	Haven't we paid our share?	Yes and no.	You have paid a share, but education is an ongoing investment.
Homeowners without children	(-)/(e & l)	Why should we pay at all?	Everyone benefits from quality education.	Everyone should contribute to educating our young people.

FIGURE 15: MESSAGE DEVELOPMENT WORKSHEET (BLANK)

AUDIENCE	EXPECTED REACTION	WHAT WILL THEY ASK?	WHAT DO WE SAY TO THEM?	BROADER IMPLICATIONS/ POSITIONING STATEMENTS

PART VI /
Four Priorities as a Spokesperson

There are four specific priorities that you should embrace as a spokesperson. In descending order of importance, these are are to:

▶ Protect yourself.

▶ Protect your organization.

▶ Answer questions.

▶ Weave in key messages at appropriate times.

It makes sense that your first priority should be to protect yourself. Nobody wants to commit a career-limiting move as a result of an interview with reporters. Closely intertwined with this is your need to protect the organization or group you represent. No organization accepts a media interview with the intent of damaging its reputation. At worst, it accepts interview requests with the intent of exercising some form of damage control. The organization would prefer to be portrayed in a positive light.

When it comes to the third priority, answering questions, it's interesting to note that performing this skill well actually enables you to protect yourself and your organization effectively. To understand this, consider what happens in a court of law when a lawyer is preparing a witness.

When a witness is being prepared to testify at a trial, the lawyer provides advice that has stood the test of time. When asked a question, the witness is counseled to pause and think before saying anything. In that pause, the witness will be encouraged to carefully examine that question and that question only. The witness will be told to answer only that question. He or she will not consider the 50 or 60 questions that could precede the actual question asked, nor will the witness think about the 200 or 300 questions that could follow. The witness does not answer a question he or she hoped would have been asked. He or she is taught to focus only on the question asked.

Next, the witness will answer that question and that question only. After answering the question, the witness will immediately stop talking. To recap, the witness is told to pause, answer and stop talking (P-A-S). This is the first tactic for print interviews that we'll examine in a moment.

Let's examine lawyers' motives for providing this advice. Do lawyers suggest that a witnesses pause, answer and stop because the lawyer wants the witness to damage his or her own credibility? No, lawyers provide such advice because they want witnesses to protect their personal credibility.

Do lawyers counsel witnesses to pause, answer and stop because they want the witness to damage the case, in a bold attempt to increase billable hours? No, if the lawyers are generating sufficient billable hours, we can safely assume they want their witnesses to protect the case and/or the organization.

Therefore, by pausing, answering and stopping, witnesses can protect themselves and their organizations in a court of law, which is arguably one of the most difficult question-and-answer exchanges that exists. If this advice works well in that environment, wouldn't it also work well to protect spokespeople and their organizations in the court of public opinion, particularly during print interviews?

By answering the question and stopping, you allow reporters to steer the process and do their job, which is to ask questions. This enables you to ultimately manage the process to a win-win for both of you.

Your job is to balance the third and fourth priorities: answering questions and finding places to weave in your messages.

PART VII /
Specific Strategies for Success

There are a number of differences between broadcast and print media; therefore, you should employ different strategies when answering questions from reporters in each type of medium.

PRINT INTERVIEWS / Because print reporters need more information than their counterparts in radio and television, they will ask more questions. As a result, print interviews tend to take longer and go into greater depth than interviews for broadcast. And in a print interview, the path to the end audience (the readers of newspapers and magazines) is always indirect. Reporters and editors stand between you and the end audiences with whom you would like to communicate.

This is why you must be clear, concise and focused during print interviews. Keep your answers short. Allow the reporter to ask more questions. There are two basic strategies to keep in mind, which are illustrated in Figure 16. The first is to pause, answer the question and stop talking (P-A-S). The second is to pause, answer the question, weave in (not drive home) a message and stop talking (P-A-W-S).

FIGURE 16: STRATEGIES FOR PRINT INTERVIEWS

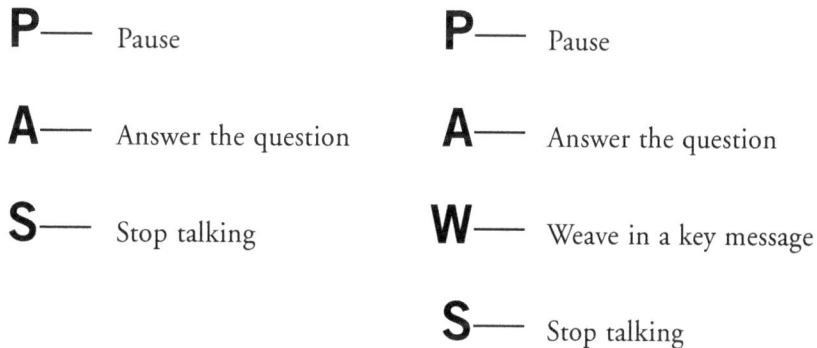

P— Pause   **P**— Pause

A— Answer the question   **A**— Answer the question

S— Stop talking   **W**— Weave in a key message

                             S— Stop talking

Your primary responsibility during print interviews is to answer questions clearly and concisely, and then stop talking. In doing so, you must attempt to adhere to the principle of "less is more."

To be successful at this, however, you must understand the difference between closed questions requiring a yes or no response and open-ended questions requiring slightly more information.

Closed questions are those requiring a short answer. This could be yes or no, but could also be possibly, potentially, under certain circumstances and never. Open-ended questions—such as why and how questions—tend to require more explanation. As you look for points in which to weave key messages, you will probably most often find them when a reporter asks open-ended questions.

Above all, remember the value of stopping after answering the question. You will have difficulty protecting yourself and your organization if you talk nonstop, especially if you talk nonstop to simple closed questions requiring a yes or no answer.

Preparation time for print interviews tends to be longer than that for broadcast interviews. Because reporters require more information, you need more information. When preparing for print interviews, bring facts, figures, data and statistics with you. Don't try to overwhelm the reporter with information but have it ready if needed.

When you do present facts, try to relate them to a human perspective. This applies to all print interviews, especially magazine interviews. Putting a human face on factual information helps make it relevant to reporters, and assists them in making that information relevant to readers.

MOVING TO BROADCAST / There are two types of broadcast interviews: sound bites for radio and television, and live interviews. The distinguishing feature between these two is that, in a sound bite, the audience will not hear the questions asked. To deal with this, you will create an answer for each question or series of questions asked that will contain the question, the answer and your message. Figure 17 illustrates the sound bite.

FIGURE 17: THE SOUND BITE

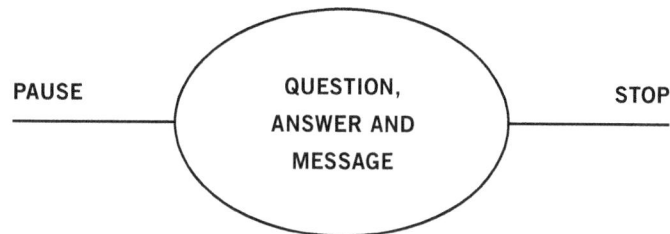

In a live interview, whether that interview is done live to air or recorded and played back later, the audience hears questions and answers together with minimal or no editing. Whether for television or radio, this format is designed to be a conversation between you and the interviewer. It's important that you answer questions wherever and whenever possible. You are there to tell a story. If your decision making is reasonable, rational and ethical, you should have no fear of the interviewer steering the shape, context and dimension of that story.

SOUND BITES

A sound bite is a short piece of information that is inserted into a story for radio or television, either in a newscast or some type of feature program. Sound bites can be 10–20 seconds in length. They are rarely longer, and are often much shorter. If you want to improve your idea of how short sound bites can be, watch a few newscasts on television with your closed captioning feature switched on. Some are as short as five or six words.

You should approach a sound bite with the goal of creating self-contained units of information for each question or series of questions asked. These units of information should be complete to the point that they stand on their own. This is important because the audience will not hear the questions asked; they will only hear your answer.

To be successful with sound bites, you should pause, restate the question and answer it (or vice-versa), weave in one appropriate message, and stop talking (P-A/R-W-S). Figure 18 illustrates this process.

In many cases, the reporter will ask you more than one question at a time before allowing you to answer. After asking one or more questions, the reporter will put a microphone in front of you and await your answers. Remember that the end audience, even in a media scrum, will probably not hear the questions asked. These are often edited out so you must take the time to think before you speak.

FIGURE 18: CREATING SOUND BITES

P— Pause

A/R— Answer the question

W— Weave in a key message

S— Stop talking

Pausing before answering also helps from a technical perspective. Those in the editing suite will be looking for a clean sound bite that they can insert into the story with minimal editing. Pausing helps this process. It also helps ensure that the microphone is in place before you start speaking. If the microphone is still moving toward you when you start talking, the sound bite will be of poor quality and will not be used.

How long can you pause? Theoretically, as long as you need to in order to think of an answer. During that pause, you're going to create a self-contained piece of information that has the question, answer and message all in one. You repeat this process for each question or series of questions asked.

It's important to recognize that you restate the question instead of re-asking it. Here are some examples to give you an idea of how this process can unfold:

Question: Do you understand how to answer and restate the question?

    A/R: Yes, I understand how to answer and restate the question.

    R/A: I understand how to answer and restate the question, yes.

    Not: Are you asking if I understand how to answer and restate the question?

Question: Why are securities investigators camped out at your financial institution?

    A/R: Securities investigators have borrowed office space at our financial instutition to execute a warrant on a company that is a client of ours.

Question: Do you think it's fair that securities investigators have borrowed office space at your institution?

A/R-W: Yes, we do think it's fair that securities investigators have borrowed office space here [insert message] because this will help us balance the needs of their investigation while protecting client privacy.

Question: Will your need to protect client privacy hamper the investigation?

A/R-W: No, our need to protect client privacy will not hamper the investigation because we will ensure they get all the information outlined in the warrant they're serving.

As you can see, the spokesperson repeats and answers each question or series of questions asked. Where the reporter engages in prejudicial language while asking a question, the spokesperson has the right to change that prejudicial language while answering and restating the question (i.e., "camped out" became "borrowed office space").

LIVE BROADCAST INTERVIEWS

In a live interview, the audience hears both the questions and the answers with minimal or no editing. This applies whether the interview is carried live on-air at the time, or recorded and played back later. This interview most closely resembles a conversation between the interviewer and you, as the spokesperson for your organization.

This is the most challenging of all interviews, and is slightly different from the others we've discussed. The first difference is that it is virtually impossible to pause during a live interview. In fact, if you do, you'll drive the interviewer crazy. He or she will not want any "dead air" after questions are asked. As the interviewer is asking the question, you must already be forming an answer. While you're doing this, you must also make sure you know what you're answering.

Since the audience hears both the question and the answer, if you don't hear the question and answer the wrong question (or you purposely ignore the question), the audience is able to form their own impressions of the exchange. Make no mistake, if you don't answer the question, the audience will know it.

During a live interview, the audience can form a general perception of you. This can potentially work for and against you. It can work for you because it is difficult to take any answer or remark that you provide out of context. Every aspect of the interview is in plain view for everyone. However, herein lies the danger. If you sidestep, waffle or evade, that too is in plain view. You may get away with it from time to time, but you can't fool everyone forever.

It is also extremely difficult to answer questions with one word during a live interview. You should answer the question as soon as possible after it is asked, and be prepared to provide context for the question or your answer. Having said this, however, keep your answers relatively short. When you've provided an idea or some context, stop talking. The interviewer, who will not like dead air, will undoubtedly ask another question.

Being proficient at live interviews takes practice. These interviews shouldn't be taken lightly, and your first interview with a reporter probably shouldn't be a live one. However, if you learn to handle live interviews effectively, you should potentially be able to handle any media challenge that comes your way.

DETERMINING WHICH SCENARIO APPLIES / Determine which scenario you're working with—print, sound bite or live interview—when you negotiate the interview with the reporter. (This is where you worked through Figure 11 on page 29). In addition to learning about potential topics, determine whether you are talking to a print or broadcast reporter. If you are to be interviewed for broadcast purposes, find out whether the reporter is looking for a sound bite or actuality (eight to 20 seconds of information for a newscast), or whether the interview will be live (in which the audience hears both the questions asked by the reporter and the answers you provide).

In each of the scenarios, the bottom line is very similar. You must find the balance that not only has you communicating through the reporter to the audiences important to your organization, but also enables you to communicate with the reporter and answer his or her questions. Indeed, the only time you should ignore the reporter's questions and focus exclusively on driving home key messages is in a highly volatile situation where the messages you convey are the only things you say "for the record." In that situation, you simply keep repeating one or two key messages, regardless of the question asked. In all other cases, however, your job as a spokesperson is to balance what the reporter is attempting to achieve (i.e., the story he or she is attempting to develop) with what your organization hopes to communicate.

☐ CONCLUSION

It's important to keep a few things in mind as you prepare to face print and broadcast reporters.

There is a difference between broadcast and print media. In print, the reporter will need more information and, as a result, will ask more questions. Interviews will be longer, and the reporter often has the time and space to show subtlies in the story. However, in print, the path to the end audience is always indirect.

Broadcast interviews tend to be shorter. Reporters require less information and, as a result, broadcast tends to portray issues from a black-and-white perspective. There is the possibility of conveying both personality and message in broadcast, and you can send messages directly to the end audience.

In their portrayal of information and issues, reporters attempt to create polarization. Your job is to keep your wits about you. Stick to your logic, and convey that logic to the reporter with clear, concise and focused answers to the reporter's questions.

Working with reporters is a challenge. They can help your organization, but they can also hurt it. Treat them like valued customers. Never provide them with anything "off the record," and recognize that you must communicate effectively to them before you can effectively communicate through them.

Negotiate and prepare for every interview. Develop your messages, but recognize that the interview may take you beyond the realm of these messages. If this occurs, you might try to bridge back to your key messages, but be sensitive to a reporter who brushes them aside and pursues another line of questioning. In that case, save your messages for another day and help the reporter do his or her job by answering each question as it is asked.

When it comes to answering questions, teach yourself the skill of pausing before responding. You can develop this skill in everyday life. You don't need to wait until your next interview with a reporter to work on it.

Don't become overly preoccupied with body language. Treat the media interview like a job interview; in other words, be on your best behavior. If you try to overly control your hand gestures or convey an image of someone other than who you are, you will not be yourself, and your message will become muddled or lost in the process.

Avoid jargon. If you have to resort to jargon, it's a signal that you are unable to answer the reporter's questions (or communicate your message) clearly and concisely. Use short, simple sentences and straightforward language.

Use examples and anecdotes if you wish, but not at the expense of keeping your answers brief. Ensure that the process is receiver-driven and allow the reporter the opportunity to do his or her job.

Finally, relax and have fun. Having a conversation with the reporter will go a long way toward getting your message across clearly, concisely and with confidence. It will help you build a relationship with that person, and this will help your organization achieve its communication goals and objectives.

ABOUT THE AUTHOR:
Eric Bergman, BPA, ABC, APR, MC, FCPRS

Eric Bergman is the world's most experienced and credentialed media training professional.

He conducted his first media relations campaign, and coached his first spokespeople, during the summer of 1981, when he promoted two student theatre productions, *Pal Joey* and *A Funny Thing Happened on the Way to the Forum*. "I gave very similar advice then to what I would give today," he says. "Relax, let the interviewer guide the process, tell the story, and make sure people know when the plays are running and how they can purchase tickets."

Eric formally started his public relations career a year later as a government public affairs officer. During his 30-plus-year career, he has worked in virtually every aspect of public relations and corporate communications. He has been self-employed since 1985.

Since 1993, his business has focused exclusively on presentation skills and media training. In the early 1990s, he developed two unique and effective communication training programs: *Present With Ease* and *At Ease With the Media*. "I developed *At Ease With the Media* to set the global standard for media training," he says. "The program is based on the highest models of excellence in communication management: win-win outcomes."

Eric holds a bachelor of professional arts (BPA) in communication studies from Athabasca University and a two-year diploma in advertising and public relations from Grant MacEwan University.

He is an accredited business communicator (ABC), an accredited public relations practitioner (APR), and a master communicator (MC), which is the highest distinction that can be bestowed upon a Canadian member of the International Association of Business Communicators. In 2014, he was named a member of the College of Fellows of the Canadian Public Relations Society (FCPRS).